Why I Am a Conscientious Objector

Other Books by John M. Drescher

Follow Me (Herald Press)
If I Were Starting My Family Again (Abingdon)
Meditations for the Newly Married (Herald Press)
Now Is the Time to Love (Herald Press)
Seven Things Children Need (Herald Press)
Spirit Fruit (Herald Press)
The Way of the Cross and Resurrection, editor
   (Herald Press)
What Should Parents Expect? (Abingdon)
When Opposites Attract (Abbey Press)
You Can Plan a Good Marriage (Baker)
When You Think You Are in Love (Abbey Press)

John M. Drescher Visitation Pamphlets (Herald Press)

Blessings by Your Bedside
By Still Waters
Facing Illness with Faith
For the Golden Years
I Lift My Eyes
In Grief's Slow Hour
May Your Marriage Be a Happy One
Personal Prescriptions
Sources of Spiritual Strength
Spiritual Nutrients
Strength for Suffering
Suffering and God's Presence

Why I Am a Conscientious Objector

A Christian Peace Shelf Selection

John M. Drescher
Introduction by Myron S. Augsburger

HERALD PRESS
Scottdale, Pennsylvania
Kitchener, Ontario

Library of Congress Cataloging in Publication Data

Drescher, John M.
  Why I am a conscientious objector.

  Bibliography: p.
  1. Peace (Theology) I. Title.
BT736.4.D66   261.8'73   82-894
ISBN 0-8361-1993-2 (pbk.)   AACR2

Portions of this book are adapted and expanded by permission from
the author's article, "Why Christians Shouldn't Carry Swords,"
Christianity Today, November 7, 1980.

WHY I AM A CONSCIENTIOUS OBJECTOR
Copyright © 1982 by Herald Press, Scottdale, Pa. 15683
  Published simultaneously in Canada by Herald Press,
  Kitchener, Ont. N2G 4M5
Library of Congress Catalog Card Number: 82-894
International Standard Book Number: 0-8361-1993-2
Printed in the United States of America
Design: Alice B. Shetler

  83 84 85 86 87 10 9 8 7 6 5 4 3 2

To all those who,
because they seek to follow Christ,
choose another way.

Contents

Contents

Author's Preface

Many books and pamphlets (including scholarly works, historical and biblical studies) are available on the subject of the relation of the Christian and war. A bibliography of some of these begins on page 65.

This booklet is not a defense of a position so much as the sharing of my own search and stance on the issue of the relationship of the Christian to warfare. Here I look at the broad yet basic issues I believe every Christian must consider when confronted with military involvements. This is also a kind of summary of what many Christians have held since the beginning of Christianity. Additional reading on all these issues can be found in the bibliography.

May God bless the truths of these pages for his own glory and the good of those who read.

John M. Drescher
Harrisonburg, Virginia

Introduction

God has disarmed the Christian. He has called us into a new community which has its citizenship in heaven. This is our first loyalty, our primary relationship. Having been disarmed by God, we lay aside guns and bombs because they are too weak to achieve his goals.

We are called to love, to live by love, to share in the redemptive mission of Christ. As Christians we are armed with love, believing that love is the one valid way to conquer enemies. As God has loved his enemies in acting redemptively for them, so the child of God is called to love all persons and to call them into the fellowship of faith. In this fellowship Christians have more in common with fellow Christians across national lines than with non-Christian fellow citizens. As with Abraham, we also are called to abandon all for the "city whose builder and maker is God."

In this book John Drescher unapologetically shares his conviction and the biblical basis for an evangelical pacifism. He presents a clear call for Christians to give priority to the life of Christ as a way of peace. Fully aware that we do not expect nations to follow the path of discipleship, the author challenges Christians to choose peace and to work for peace among the nations. He sets peacemaking in the context of our evangelical mission to win all persons, including our enemies, to become our brothers and sisters in Christ.

The great issues facing us in the world today are poverty, race, and war. As Christians we are called to relate the message of the kingdom of God to each of these. This message is one of love and peace, a call to social change by relationship with Jesus. Our crucial word for a troubled world is that the risen Christ is *the liberator,* that he modeled in his nonviolence the way to a new community. As Martin Luther King said, "The choice is no longer between violence and nonviolence. It is either nonviolence or nonexistence."

If ever Marshall McLuhan's words "The medium is the message," were true, it is when the way of love communicates the love of Christ. This is a desperately needed message in a day of the worship of power—that which Malcolm Muggeridge has called a "pornography of the will." The words of Jesus are most relevant, "Blessed are the meek . . ." for they are the ones who actually enjoy the earth. "Blessed are the peacemakers . . ." for they are expressing their participation in the family of God.

The question all of us must raise is, If God has disarmed the Christian, on whose authority does a Christian pick up arms again? The answer Drescher gives is clear: No authority can supersede that of God. Those who would render this role to Caesar need to answer the question of how a government, any government, can countermand God. And those who see violence as evil, but an inescapable evil for which we ask God's forgiveness, will need to answer how those who take up arms against God's will can presume on his forgiveness. And for those who find occasion to declare a given war to be a "just war," the issue should at least be arrived at through larger Christian consensus and not left to the private judgment of individuals. The Christian convictions and biblical evidence presented by this author must be a part of the dialogue.

Peace is an important concern for all of humanity. In fact, with 50,000 nuclear warheads in place—enough to blow the world to pieces fifty times over—peace is the overriding social-political issue of this decade. In addition to our concern over who might push the button, we should find the way for the button not to exist. But as Christians we know that peace is more than disarmament, more than the absence of terror. It is the shalom from God, the well-being of a people living in grace. Our mission is to extend the love of Christ, to expand the community of God's people, to enhance the transnational fellowship of the Spirit.

"For he is our peace, who hath made both one, and hath broken down the middle wall of partition between us" (Ephesians 2:14). Let us pray that the dynamic of Christ's love in the lives of conscientious Christians will become a powerful force for peace in our threatened world.

Myron S. Augsburger
Washington, D.C.

1

A Starting Point

1
A Starting Point

My college roommate, several years after World War II, was a dedicated young German of my own denomination. He had served in Hitler's army. In our late night discussions he described how he and other German Christians were caught up in all the fervor and fury of German patriotism. During those war years he never doubted he was doing his God-given duty. He was confident that the German cause was just and he could not believe anything to the contrary. Those who thought otherwise were traitors. After all, the German war slogan was "God is with us."

Along the frontier of Germany and France one can see tombstones bearing the identical inscription: "For God and the Fatherland." Some are in French, marking the graves of those who died fighting for France; some are in German, over those who died fighting for Germany. Troops from both countries included persons claiming to be Christians, who believed God was on their side as they battled each other. Both sides believed their nation was waging a just war. And both obeyed without question the demands of political and religious leaders who assured them they were right in doing so.

Such troubling facts led me to study seriously what the Scripture says on the Christian's relation to war. I needed to deal honestly with whether the position of those who seek to follow Jesus should be different from those who do not.

Further I was forced to look at the practice of the church down through the centuries and draw conclusions from such a study. Is the church part and parcel of the world when it comes to war or does the church of Jesus Christ have a different message and method in dealing with conflict?

In sharing the essence of my own conviction as a Christian conscientious objector to war I bear witness to what Scripture, the Holy Spirit, and the convictions of many other concerned and committed Christians say to me. I believe my position corresponds closely with the viewpoint of persons and churches who have adhered to the Christian peace position down through the centuries. And I find that in nearly every denomination or church tradition, in every generation, some persons believed and preserved the views commonly held by those called "peace churches."

In sharing my personal convictions as a conscientious objector to participation in war, I recognize that the subject is one which has divided sincere Christians since the fourth century. Prior to that time there was almost unanimous agreement that Christians cannot engage in warfare. Since then there have been many attempts at reconciling Christianity and war.

My Position

Briefly stated biblical pacifism is rooted in divine revelation. It accepts the Scripture as final authority in all matters of faith and conduct. Its frame of reference is biblical rather than philosophical or historical. It views the New Testament as God's fullest revelation with Christ at the center as the final court of appeal. Here is where the Christian must begin in discussing Christian ethical behavior.

Further biblical pacifism is rooted in the experience of the new birth by the Word and Holy Spirit. Its practice cannot be expected from persons who operate only on the human level with human strength alone.

Biblical or Christian pacifism, in its very essence, takes the Scripture, Christ, regeneration, and the church with utmost seriousness. While other forms of pacifism may contain important and helpful truths, biblical pacifism is different in its orientation.

Kinds of Pacifism

Humanistic pacifism places primary emphasis on what concerned persons can do and applies a peace ethic to all society. It despises war primarily because of war's destructive nature upon both humanity and all life's resources.

Gandhian pacifism exerts pressure by peaceful means to accomplish desired ends. It is rightly concerned about human welfare. On one occasion, when Calcutta was seething with riots and bloodshed between Muslims and Hindus, Gandhi with love and without violence went to the center of the dangerous city and peace was restored. What thousands of armed soldiers could not do, one man committed to peace did.

Moralistic pacifism makes much of the immorality of

war and the dignity and goodness of mankind. It appeals to people's moral judgment on war and the issues involved.

Political pacifism proposes political action, law, and pressure upon government to avoid war. This approach seeks to entrench itself in government to guide the state in the avoidance of war.

Anarchistic pacifism repudiates or rejects government. It says the state is evil.

Apocalyptic pacifism perceives the possibility for peace and the practice of Jesus' teaching in love only in some future age when there will be no enemies or weapons of war. It sees Christ's commands on love and peace as impractical and impossible at present. Others take a position which looks to the future in the reverse of this. They refuse carnal weapons now but believe that in the final great war, God's war, in which they will share, the weapons God does not now allow will be approved, as they join in the final battle.

Different Approaches

A quick survey of approaches by those who to one degree or another sanction the Christian engaging in warfare might be summarized as follows:

The Catholic Church generally has assumed two layers of Christian piety. The clergy in obedience to the Scripture dare not fight in war, but the laypeople who are not expected to live in such holy devotion may fight. The grace of the holy persons somehow covers those who fight.

Modern fundamentalism calls for unquestioning obedience to earthly rulers in this area, while usually claiming a clean break in other areas. They depend heavily on Old Testament illustrations and appeal strongly to church tradition and a literalistic interpretation of Christ as the lion, warrior, or the conqueror.

An approach taken largely by the more *liberal wing of Christendom* begins with the fact of sin rather than with Christ and points to the Christian's responsibility in society. Being part of sinful humanity, the Christian carries social responsibility. Since all of us are both good and evil, we all are involved in the sin-stained society. A part of that sin is conflict. The Christian must, in times of war, judge which is the greater evil and choose the lesser. This may mean fighting in some wars but refusing to fight in others.

The Just War Theory

Much of Christendom, across denominational lines Catholic and Protestant, has attempted to deal with the Christian's participation in war on the basis of the "just war" theory. This theory says that under certain strictly-adhered-to conditions, a particular war might be an exception to the gospel and not a violation of the New Testament teaching. The following four criteria are to guide Christians on whether or not to participate in a specific war:

1. War is permissible only after all other efforts have failed.

2. The intention of the war must be good. For example, it should be for the restoration of law and order, not for economic or exploitive advantage of any kind.

3. There must be no burning, massacre, or killing of innocent victims. Targets must be military, not civilian.

4. The force used in war must be proportionate to the goal sought. War should not destroy more than is gained.

According to the "just war" theory Christians are to apply these criteria in every war. And if the conditions or intentions of the war change, Christians must declare the war is wrong and a violation of the gospel and refuse to fight.

In response, several observations are in order. First, the theory has never worked. There is no record that it was ever used. Since its conception in the fourth century it has remained only a theory. Never has a body of bishops or major denominational body officially condemned any war.

Second, it assumes that one side will be just and the other unjust. But as we know, both sides claim their cause is just in times of war. Obviously there is much that is unjust on both sides and no nation is an unbiased judge of the moral rightness of its cause.

Catholic writer Richard McSorley in *Kill? for Peace?* states another weakness: "The theory was formulated to show that *some* wars might be an exception to the law of the gospel; it has become a theory used to justify *every* war that comes along. Instead of justifying an exceptional war, it is used to make all wars acceptable. . . .

"The just war theory is the only attempt at a moral justification of war by Christians. If it is rejected, then the Christian is left with the gospel, which rejects killing as immoral."

Further the "just war" theory implies (1) that a nation will truthfully present all the facts to its people before and during a war so that the Christian can make a moral judgment, and (2) that the Christian, usually an 18-year-old person, has the discernment to make a correct judgment.

Finally, many Christians who previously held to the "just war" theory admit that it breaks down completely, if indeed it ever could be used, when modern weapons are designed indiscriminately to destroy masses of civilians. Bede Griffith in *Morals and Missiles*, Catholic essays on the problem of war, writes: "Until now it has been a matter of debate whether it is legitimate for a Christian to refuse to fight, but now the question must be whether it is legitimate for a Christian to fight at all." Modern warfare technology alone has rendered the "just war" theory obsolete.

Nonresistance

The biblical pacifism position holds that those who submit unconditionally to the lordship of Christ in faith and life cannot morally participate in any war. Accepting Christ, his teaching, his life, and his cross as our final frame of reference points clearly to laying down one's own life rather than taking the life even of an enemy. The doctrine of biblical nonresistance does not rest on a few proof texts but rather is vitally related to the very essence of the gospel, the regenerated nature of the Christian, and the lordship of Christ.

Biblical pacifism is the result of Christian discipleship. My refusal to fight is based upon my calling as Christ's disciple. Jesus is my Lord! He is my teacher and I am determined to follow in his steps obediently, regardless of the consequences. My way of life and ethics must be in harmony with his. As the way of salvation is determined by him, not by me, so the way I am called to live is determined by his standards, not mine. Christ tells us to love our enemies, pray for our enemies, forgive our enemies, do good to our enemies, and overcome evil with good.

Biblical pacifism's objective is to lead others to know Christ and to follow him, helping them find reconciliation with God and others so that they in turn can become ministers of the gospel of reconciliation. To do this it is impossible to participate in any program of ill will, retaliation, or war which conflicts with Christ's spirit and commands. Having stated my sincere views concerning the Christian engaging in warfare, let me enlarge on several basic areas of conviction as a conscientious objector.

2
The Victorious Christ

2

The Victorious Christ

First and fundamental to my position is my understanding of who Christ is, what he says, and what he did.

Who He Is
The beginning point in my conscientious objection to war has to do with *who Christ is*. He is the "word become flesh." He is the one through whom God has spoken in these last days. Christ is God's will incarnate. He is the full and final message of God's will and of what he intends us, as his people, to be. We are called "to be as he is in the world."

A clear and constant concern of Scripture is to present Christ as the cosmic Christ. He is the Savior of the world. He died for all and cares equally for each person. But we love to localize him. We regard Christ as a respecter of persons, and demand that he become a national, denominational, or personal God only. Especially during wartime, in spite of our confessions of faith, we limit his love.

In wartime it seems difficult to believe that Christ died to save our enemies as much as he died for us. We try to confine Christ in the small container of one country. But Christ cannot be thus confined. He has called and is calling disciples from every tribe, tongue, and nation. He is the Christ of all cultures. He is not on the side of the biggest bomb. He will never sanction belief in racial superiority, the sin of cultural pride, or the destruction of others of his children. As the cosmic Christ, the Savior of the world, he cannot.

What He Says

My Christology must further take into account, not only what Christ is, but *what he says*. Jesus declared, "I am the way, the truth, and the life." To believe this is to accept him not only as the way to God for salvation, but to accept his teachings as the way of daily discipleship. So I seek to live under his lordship. He is the authority for belief and behavior even though the temptation remains to live a life and to use methods he never allowed and even spoke against.

This means that I do not go to the Old Testament as my primary reference to prove the rightness of warfare any more than I go to the Old Testament to prove the rightness of polygamy, slavery, or animal sacrifices. Christ came to fulfill the law in his own life and in his teaching. His "but I say unto you" supersedes the Old Testament statements and especially the reports of Old Testament behavior. Thus reports of Joshua's battles do not become the basis of belief and behavior for the New Testament believer. Nor does the Christian derive his doctrine of war and peace from the account of David's destruction of Goliath and his killing of ten thousands.

To take seriously the truth that Jesus is God's final message means that I cannot add "except" to Christ's commands. I dare not say, "Love your enemies (except in wartime)"; "Do not resist an evil person (except in wartime)"; "Put your sword back in its place . . . for all who draw the sword will die by the sword (except when the government tells one to fight)"; "If anyone says, 'I love God,' yet hates his brother, he is a liar (except when he fights a war)"; "Bless those who persecute you; bless and do not curse (except when my country is at war)"; "Do not take revenge . . . but leave room for God's wrath (except when Caesar says differently)"; "If your enemy is hungry, feed him (except when at war)"; and "Overcome evil with good (except when your country reverses it)."°

Christ's teaching on nonresistance to evil (on a physical level) are clear and unequivocal. They are so clear that such men as Tolstoy and Gandhi, who were not prepared to accept the total Christian gospel, found their basis for pacifism in Christ's teaching. D. L. Moody said, "There has never been a time in my life when I felt that I could take a gun and shoot down a fellow being. In this respect I am a Quaker."

Some time ago a brilliant young man at a leading university, who had no contact with the teaching of the peace churches, was asked the basis for his conscientious objection to war. He replied, "Is there any alternative for one who takes Christ's teaching and example seriously?"

One of the striking things about many who claim a high view of inspiration and biblical authority, as well as the centrality of Christ, is that they suddenly shift to philosophy, tradition, and expediency when it comes to

---

° Matthew 5:44, 39; 26:52; 1 John 4:20; Romans 12:14, 19, 20, 21.

the war question. Many appeal far more to tradition and the words of church fathers than they do to the Scripture. Unlike their decisive appeal to the New Testament for conversion and standards of Christian behavior in other areas, they appeal to the Old Testament for the sanction of Christians engaging in warfare.

William C. Allen describes the discrepancy between the Christian engaging in warfare and the teaching of Christ thus: "When I heard the sergeant who called out to the lads fresh from bayonet practice, while instructing them how to stab and cut at the vitals of the enemy, 'Now boys, you must forget all that you learned in Sunday school,' I realized that the Sunday school teaches one thing and the army another."

A writer in the *Christliche Welt*, a prominent religious journal in Germany in 1917, proposed the temporary suspension of Christianity for the duration of the World War. "In a war of this character, where ruthlessnesses of an unparalleled type are displayed and when the very rudiments of Christianity are ignored, it would be wise," the journal suggested, "if Christianity is to be maintained, that it should not be preached, or taught, during the continuance of war."

Jonathan Dymond in *Essay on War* (1824) wrote: "If we will not be peaceable, let us then at least be honest, and acknowledge that we continue to slaughter one another, not because Christianity permits it, but because we reject her laws."

James Russell Lowell was blunt and burning in his stanza:

> *As for war, I call it murder,*
> *There you hev it plain and flat,*

I don't want to go no furder
Than my Testament fer that.

Christ will never send his disciples where he himself
will not lead. "Follow me" is forever his watchword. It is
impossible to imagine Christ leading in the slaughter of
others for whom he died.

What He Did

Finally, my Christology must take seriously *what
Christ did*. All the records of Christ's works indicate that
he spent his life in matters related to God's will and his redemptive work. One thing upon which we all agree is
that Jesus personified in his person and relationships—in
his love for his enemies by dying on a cross—the way of
love and peace. To my knowledge, no one has ever dared
to picture Christ with a gun in his hand.

Jesus is my example. He demonstrated throughout his
earthly life the way of suffering love in contrast to retaliation. All Christ's words are brought to living expression in
himself. And he says, "As the Father has sent me, I am
sending you" (John 20:21). The Scripture repeatedly says
in many different ways, "As he is, so am I in this present
world."

According to the apostles, the way Christ dealt with
evil and how he bore his cross instead of retaliating
against his enemies are to be imitated. All the New Testament writers, with the possible exception of Jude, men-
tion this. Paul says, "Follow me as I follow Christ." Peter
points out clearly, "To this you were called, because
Christ suffered for you, leaving you an example, that you
should follow in his steps.... When they hurled their in-
sults at him, he did not retaliate; when he suffered, he

made no threats. Instead, he entrusted himself to him who judges justly" (1 Peter 2:21, 23) "Whoever claims to live in him [Jesus] must walk as Jesus did" (1 John 2:6). Paul writes, "Your attitude should be the same as that of Christ Jesus" (Philippians 2:5).

Christ demonstrated the way of peace, and he commands his followers to do the same. We are to have his spirit in relating to our enemies. "If anyone does not have the Spirit of Christ, he does not belong to Christ" (Romans 8:9). The Sermon on the Mount, the essence of Jesus' teaching, is picked up phrase by phrase throughout the New Testament, calling for obedience here and now. As a peacemaker, Christ calls me to invade and penetrate all of life and society—with life, not death—and to preach the practical possibility of reconciliation among persons everywhere. I witness by what I say and do that the war is over, that hostility is an outright denial of the message of Christ, contrary to the spirit of his teaching. "Jesus said, 'My kingdom is not of this world. If it were, my servants would fight.... But now my kingdom is from another place" (John 18:36).

Relation to the Cross

To make Christ only divine in dying for us and then to claim that we are not to live as he lived, not to follow in his steps, is to fall into the old docetic heresy which denies Christ's true humanity. Christ calls us not only to enter into his death but to live his life. The new birth is not only a rebirth of the soul but a rebirth of life where all things become new. And his Holy Spirit is given to us to bring to pass the divine will in us.

C. G. Rutenber of Eastern Baptist Seminary commenting on the song, "Battle Hymn of the Republic" says,

"That typical war song of Christendom, dragging Christ to battle, needs to have the sentimentality squeezed out of it. Realistically, it must be read like this: 'As he died to make man holy, let us kill to make men free.' Also that spoils the song."

The great betrayal of Christ through the centuries is that his professed followers reach out to claim the benefits of the cross for salvation but refuse to take the way of the cross as the means to live the Christ life. Christ calls us not only to faith but to discipleship. The way of the cross is always linked to the work of the cross. The whole life and death of Christ is an indictment of carnal warfare.

Christ's disciples were slow at learning that his methods were opposite the sword. When Peter felt he could solve things by using the sword Jesus had to remind him that this is not the way his kingdom operates (John 18:10-11).

I agree with Reo M. Christenson, who wrote in *Christianity Today* (January 5, 1973): "It still seems reasonable to me that the church should condemn such public evils as racial discrimination, cruelty, oppression, hypocrisy, deceit, corruption, and war—especially war, which I find wholly incompatible with the Sermon on the Mount and all Jesus stood for. And I think the church should encourage its members to oppose these things by every peaceful and ethical means. All of these are evils that Jesus opposed by word, example, implicitly, and explicitly." I agree also with Robert McAfee Brown in his book *The Bible Speaks to You* when he writes, "Nothing in Jesus' life or teachings can be 'twisted' in support of killing or warfare."

Ronald J. Sider, in an outstanding article, "A Call for Evangelical Nonviolence," makes an appeal to those who take the Scripture and the atonement of Christ seriously. "It is my contention that a biblical understanding of the cross leads necessarily to a nonviolent stance, and, conversely, that only a fully biblical view of the cross and justification can provide an adequate foundation for nonviolence. As Dale Brown suggests, 'The tendency to separate God's love of his enemies from our love of [our] enemies is one of the heresies of the doctrine of the atonement.' "[1]

Scriptural Authority

Sider says further, "If evangelicals really believe that Jesus is Lord and that canonical Scripture is binding then surely there is only one possibility. If Scripture calls us to love our enemies as Jesus loved his enemies on the cross, we must either accept the way of nonviolence or abandon our affirmation of scriptural authority.... If we reject the biblical imperative to follow Jesus at this point, we in effect express our disbelief about the validity of God's way of reconciling enemies. But to do that is to express disbelief about the atonement itself."[2]

Thus to take up the sword is for me to deny all Christ is, what he said, and what he did in life and in dying on the cross.

1. Dale W. Brown, *Brethren and Pacifism* (Elgin, Ill.: Brethren Press, 1970), p. 121.

2. Ronald J. Sider in *The Christian Century*, September 15, 1976.

3
The Global Gospel

3

The Global Gospel

Fundamental to my peace position is my understanding of the gospel. The entire New Testament teaches that the gospel is global. One distinguished advocate of world missions wrote, "Nothing is more deeply embedded in Christianity than its universality." The gospel is to be preached to every creature.

The reconciling work of Christ cannot be restricted to one community, church, country, or continent. The gospel is the good news of one who, rather than following the world's way of righting wrongs, gave himself for the wrongdoers.

J. B. Phillips paraphrases Paul's statement in Ephesians 2:16, 17, "For he reconciled both [Jew and Greek, insider and outsider] to God by the sacrifice of one body on the cross, and by this act made utterly irrelevant the antagonism between them. Then he came and told both you who were far from God [the outsiders, the Gentiles] and us who were near [the insiders, the Jews] that the war was over." That is the gospel: war is not only sin, but war for the believer is over.

That is the good news. For me as a Christian all persons loved by God are my beloved also—even though they may consider me their enemy. Redeeming love is at the heart of the gospel; love and peace are God's plan for people regardless of who they are. For me to participate in warfare means that I go contrary to all I understand the gospel to mean.

Richard C. Detweiler wrote: "To preach a gospel of reconciliation while at the same time supporting or even participating in military action as the will of God is the height of contradiction. The same must be said with regard to the Christian's attitude toward other social evils. Whenever the means by which we witness is inconsistent with the way of the cross we profess to follow, we are contradicting our message."

War offers death instead of life, hate instead of love, judgment instead of forgiveness, retaliation rather than reconciliation; it sets out to search and destroy instead of to seek and save. It aims lethal weapons against the very persons I'm told to give the gospel. To me, engaging in warfare is the supreme denial of the Great Commission and all Christ said and did. I agree with Charles Clayton Morrison who said, "Nothing more antithetical to Christianity can be imagined than war. It is the denial in the boldest possible form of the very life principle of the religion of Jesus. It is anti-Christian in the rawest, nakedest form."

Discipleship and Evangelism

Engaging in warfare strikes at the heart of discipleship and evangelism. Each person I face in combat is either a

Christian or non-Christian. If I destroy a Christian, I kill the brother for whom Scripture says I should lay down my life. If my enemy is a non-Christian, I destroy one for whom Christ died and take away any further opportunity to be a reconciler or to let him find salvation. In the interest of the gospel and salvation, I cannot participate in war.

The supreme duty of Christians, individually and corporately, is to carry out the Great Commission. Just as nations send soldiers to the ends of the earth to destroy, so Christ commands his followers to go to the end of the world to save. War, supported by Christians, is one of the chief reasons for failure in world evangelization.

"For God was pleased to have all his fullness dwell in [Christ] . . . and through him to reconcile to himself all things, whether things on earth or things in heaven, by making peace through his blood, shed on the cross" (Colossians 1:19-20). "All this is from God, who reconciled us to himself through Christ and gave us the ministry of reconciliation: that God was reconciling the world to himself in Christ. . . . We are therefore Christ's ambassadors, as though God were making his appeal through us. We implore you on Christ's behalf: Be reconciled to God" (2 Corinthians 5:18-20).

Julia B. Foraker in *I Would Live It Again* writes of Grenville Moody, a popular army chaplain during the civil war. Chaplain Moody could easily forget the cloth, when deemed necessary, and do it with evangelistic zeal. At Lookout Mountain, for example, the colonel of Moody's regiment went tearing up and down the lines yelling to the troops, "Give 'em hell, boys! Give 'em hell!" The chaplain was at his heels yelling, "Do as your colonel tells you, boys! Do as your colonel tells you!"

Chaplain Moody accurately reflected the position of the church at large since the fourth century. In the same spirit, many who claim to represent Christ and his gospel forget his words in wartime and merely echo, often with evangelistic fervor, those who command exactly the opposite of what Christ himself commands. It stands to reason that one cannot "give 'em hell" and at the same time preach salvation. Even Frederick the Great said, "If my soldiers would really think, not one of them would remain in the ranks."

Nothing in war can be harmonized with the spirit and gospel of Jesus. A Christian engaged in war is a complete contradiction. Major General John F. O'Ryan wrote, "War is the denial of Christianity and all the most sacred things of life."

4

The Universal Church

4

The Universal Church

Fundamental to my peace position is my understanding of the church. Scripture recognizes the existence of nations. The Bible says that out of every tribe and tongue, people and nation, God gathers and redeems men and women as his people, his family, Christ's body on earth, the church. We have been brought into the kingdom of his son (Colossians 1:13). "You are a chosen people, a royal priesthood, a holy nation, a people belonging to God" (1 Peter 2:9).

Thus the nation to which the Christian belongs first is the nation over which Christ is king: it is the church of Jesus Christ. That nation exists under every form of government. Christians relate to each other regardless of race, country, or political system. This unity in Christ bridges all that separates and it breaks down all barriers. The church is "one body" (1 Corinthians 12:12, 13).

The entire New Testament teaches that the church is an interracial, supranational, transcultural body composed of all who put their faith in Jesus Christ as Savior and follow him as Lord. When one group including Christians takes up arms against another group including Christians, both are saying that Caesar, not Jesus, is Lord. Christians of one land battle and kill Christians of another land because these are requirements of nations at war; Caesar commands it. Persons in one church family put to death persons of that same church family.

William C. Allen in the *Reformed Church Messenger* writes, "When war involves Methodists stabbing Methodists, Baptists shooting Baptists, Presbyterians blowing Presbyterians to bits, Catholics anniliating Catholics, when these beastly deeds are performed at the behest of a physically safe leadership, generated for gain but hid in a propaganda of professedly noble ideals, then I am sure that war is contrary to Christian principles."

Church Unity

It is striking to me that in the great cry for church unity and oneness, not much is made of the great division and death that war brings to the body of Christ. Christians yield to the state's demand for closer solidarity in the secular struggle rather than responding to the inward and genuine call to unity in Christ across cultures and curtains. The church thus becomes representative of some select form of Christianity (American, British, or whatever) bearing more the marks of a culture or country than of the cross of Christ and of a universal fellowship where there is neither black nor white, Easterner nor Westerner, American nor Russian. The church sings, "We are not divided, all one body we," until wartime, when each church backs whatever territory it happens to be in.

44

On an existential level, this means that the body of the nation dare not be rent, but the body of Christ may be. It assumes that nation, not church, is the "destiny" man cannot escape.

I agree with Frenchman Jean Lasserre in *War and the Gospel:* "It would seem impossible for a French believer, on the grounds that his government was in conflict with the German government, to resign himself to taking part in the slaughter of Germans, when there are believers among them who, like him, form part of Christ's body." E. A. Lawrence wrote:

"The church is a gold coin of divine minting. One side shows the likeness of its Lord, the other the map of the world. Both sides are so indelibly stamped into the coin that to mar either means loss, to efface either destroys the coin.

Many of the church's songs in every land center around the scriptural idea of the church being "one body" with "one mission" and "one destiny" and yet we say all this does not apply when one nation declares war against another.

An editorial in the *Christian Century* puts it bluntly: "The church shall acknowledge the fundamental and eternal contradiction between war and Christianity; that the very fact of war shouts the failure of Christianity; and that the church therefore cannot bless war without surrendering its character as Christian. The church's clear duty therefore is to excommunicate war, deliberately and solemnly to say it, and so to inform the state, that the state may never again expect to receive the resources of the church as aids of any war in which it may ask its citizens to engage."

Over the years the church has sung:

For not with swords loud clashing
Nor roll of stirring drum,
But deeds of love and mercy,
Thy heavenly kingdom comes.

Yet the church does not have the nerve to believe this. Frederick A. Atkings wrote following World War II, "The attitude of the churches to war is so incredibly weak and illogical that it cannot be maintained much longer. The church is against war when there is no war going on; immediately when a war starts, the church blesses and supports it. War is wrong but it is perfectly justified as soon as we engage in it." Harvey Cox has written, "A church that is not able to take a firm stand against war is not a church which deserves to be believed."

War does strange things to persons. As John Haynes Holmes noted many years ago, "When a war is 'on' it is almost a hopeless task to find men who can discuss it rationally.... Reason flies out of the window along with some other valuable human assets. We are all assured that the enemy has not one virtue left, and that we have not one vice in our midst." Falsehood, hate, and bitterness take over. Preachers who proclaim love and peace in peacetime turn to preaching hate in wartime.

In his book, *Preachers Present Arms*, Ray H. Abrams documents at length the story of the involvement of the clergy in World Wars I and II as well as the Vietnam War. One minister told his people, "We are fighting not only for our country and for the democracy of the world but for the kingdom of God.... We cannot draw the line between Christianity and the military. The two go together. Every church should be a recruiting station."

Evangelist Billy Sunday in wartime suddenly shifted

from his usual theme of the love of God and salvation for all to say, "The man who breaks all the rules but at last dies fighting in the trenches is better than you God-forsaken mutts who won't enlist."

Frederick Lynch wonders how it is possible for persons reared in Christian schools and churches suddenly to make a complete turnabout to kill and shout for blood when the government and press tell them to hate. In one day all the previous teaching is forgotten, and if one dares people to remember what they were taught he is hooted down. "Is it that the human heart is too desperately wicked for even Christianity to control it when the deepest passion of all, revenge and lust for blood, are aroused?" Lynch asks.

Historian Philip V. N. Meyers, speaking to a Methodist ministers' conference, deplored the fact that "in war every soldier must bid adieu to his personal moral conscience. His moral conscience which teaches him that manslaughter in peace is murder, must in war give way to a new law, the law of loyalty to the state. The individual conscience is superseded by a supposedly higher type of war morality."

A Safe Church

C. G. Rutenber, professor of the philosophy of religion at Eastern Baptist Seminary wrote an excellent book, *The Dagger and the Cross*. In it he says, "The church always wants to be on the safe side, like the man who wears both belt and suspenders. It wants God, but it wants guns too. It wants Bibles, but it also wants bullets. It trusts in Jesus, but also in jets. And the result? The effort to mate the point of the dagger and the foot of the cross fails. Spiritual power and national, worldly power refuse to combine in stable equilibrium. The enthusiasm for battleships devours the enthusiasm for friendships. The preference for bombing missions absorbs the interest in foreign missions. Evangelism succumbs to militarism and exists only as a side issue to the successful prosecution of the war. The church becomes the handmaiden of the warrior-state."

I sense kinship with Christopher Butler who wrote in *The Catholic Worker,* "Let us take the opportunity of saying clearly that the church, the people of God, does not seek protection from its enemies—whoever they may be—in war, and especially not in war of modern type. We are the mystical body, and Christ is our Head. He refused to defend himself and his mission by the swords of his disciples or even the legions of angels, the ministers of God's justice and love. The weapons of the gospel are not nuclear but spiritual; it wins its victories not by war but by suffering."

Following World War I David Lloyd George wrote, "If there is another war, the Christian church will be responsible for it." And General Tasker Bliss said, "The responsibility is entirely on professing Christians in the United States. If another war should come they would be responsible for every drop of blood."

It is an awful condemnation on America, identified as Christian by the world, that it is considered a warring country, having killed more people in this century than most of the other nations in all of human history.

For me, therefore, I must acknowledge the tremendous eternal contradiction between war and Christianity. The church cannot bless war without surrendering its character as Christian.

5
The "Ordained" Government

5

The "Ordained" Government

Fundamental to my peace position is my understanding of what the Scripture says about government and human authority.

The Lambeth Conference in London in 1920 said, "Each of us belongs by his birth to some one of the many nations of the world. But the Christian belongs by the second birth to one holy nation which is God's own possession. When loyalty to his own nation causes conflict with the loyalty to that holy nation of which Christ is king, a Christian can have no doubt which loyalty gives way."

Basic to my not engaging in warfare is my understanding of the clear and consistent scriptural teaching on the two kingdoms. Jesus said, "My kingdom is not of this world. If it were, my servants would fight" (John 18:36).

Romans Thirteen
In the context of Romans 13 which speaks of the Chris-

tian being nonconformed to this world, living in peace, exercising love for the enemy, and leaving vengeance to God, we have the statement that the "powers" are ordained by God. This statement has caused a lot of problems for some. Several things stand out clear. God planned order not chaos or anarchy. Even bad governments can, to some degree, preserve order. Second, God is over the powers. He ordained them. But this cannot mean, as some suggest, that God is morally responsible for every ruler in power. God ordained all rulers in the same way since this is addressed to Christians regardless of the country in which we live. He ordained the leaders in China the same way he ordained leaders in the United States.

God ordered or ordained government, no doubt, in much the same way he ordained marriage. He ordained that people should hallow relationships through marriage and he ordered that mankind should live in order, not anarchy. It can never mean that he puts his stamp of approval on every marriage or on every government act.

Next the Scripture says that government officials are ministers of God to the extent that they reward the good and evil according to their merits. The effectiveness of government can be measured by these two factors. The same point is made in 1 Peter 2:13, 14. Therefore, as a Christian, I should do good. Dare we argue that the Christian is told by God to do wrong if the officials order them to do so?

Here in Romans, as elsewhere in the Scripture, I am told to submit to the authorities. Notice, however, obedience and fear are reserved for God. And if that obedience to God conflicts with human authority and results in punishment or persecution, then I, along with

Christ, the apostles, and faithful disciples down through the centuries, must be willing to submit to the consequences of that disobedience.

The Scripture can never mean, as it is interpreted by many in regard to warfare, that I must do whatever any king, president, dictator, or magistrate orders. We admire Daniel for disobeying. We could not yield if a ruler demanded idol worship or ordered us to quit preaching the gospel. Many who hold that we must obey the government when it says we should fight are the quickest to tell the government when they will not obey in other areas. Why, in this one area of warfare, do so-called Christians and biblicists say we are commanded to obey without question? Why, in this one area, is there no separation of church and state?

Further, if the command of Scripture is to obey, why try war criminals who obeyed leaders without question? Then those who obeyed Hitler in killing the Jews were doing their God-given duty; then Hitler was ordained and doing God's will. No, Jesus said, "Give to Caesar what is Caesar's, and to God what is God's" (Matthew 22:21). Obedience is for God alone. The problem is that the church has usually rendered to Caesar more than his due and to God less than belongs to him.

To render the government its due or to submit to those in authority can never mean to do anything the state asks one to do and throw the guilt back on those who issue the order.

Romans 13 also tells us not to resist the powers. Does this mean we should never question or seek to change existing programs or policies of the government? Does it mean that Christians should never speak out or act in the face of injustice and evil? Hardly! It does, however, preclude the Christian's involvement in revolution and violence. There is a vast difference between witnessing to government and taking up a gun for its overthrow. The Christian is not to engage in the overthrow of governments. And we dare not be detracted by the argument that Paul appealed to Caesar for help. There is a vast difference between appealing for legal help and taking up a gun and killing a person, his family, and as many in the community and country as possible.

Thus Romans 13 (and other passages usually used to sanction the Christian engaging in warfare) really calls Christians to refuse to be squeezed into the conformist and pagan values of the world's systems so that we may be free to pledge full allegiance to God and to live under the lordship of Christ. The New Testament teaches that the loyalty and relation of the Christian to government is a limited one: to pray and honor always, to overthrow never, and to obey when not in conflict with God's will. See 1 Timothy 2:1, 2; and Acts 5:29.

Finally a biblical pacifist is a realist. He knows the power of sin. He knows that the way of reconciliation many times means death. He does not ask, "What will happen to me if I am faithful to Christ?" He knows what faithfulness cost Christ. Like his Lord, he may be faced with the accusation that he is socially irresponsible and a traitor to his nation.

Persecution and Misunderstanding

A peacemaker can expect persecution. Jesus made this clear, and he pronounced the persecuted "blessed." Sam Darcy wrote, "In the past fifty years we have arrested tens of thousands who advocated peace. Many hundreds of them were tried, fined, and imprisoned. But we have in the past hundred years never arrested, tried, or convicted even one advocate of war."

Sometimes pacifists have been labeled cowards. The best answer to that is the courage and suffering which many pacifists have endured. And, which is easier for any of us, to go with the tide or to have the courage to stand for what one believes in spite of public opinion? Pacifism is not easy when the church, community, and the entire country is against the few who go contrary to the crowd. During the past wars, many Christian pacifists have suffered greatly, not only from government, but even more from other "Christians." One needs only to read a book such as *Peace Be with You* by Cornelia Lehn to catch a glimpse of this.

A peacemaker can expect to be misunderstood. W. G. Peck in *The Divine Revelation* writes, "The power of the world, founded upon force and forging even more perfect weapons of death, will always disown him [Jesus] as impossible." It will also disown his faithful followers. Robert E. Goodrich, Jr., speaks of a cartoon which pictures a young man on a street corner holding a sign with only one word on it—"Peace." Across the street people are yelling in hate, "Troublemaker." Goodrich comments, "The same thing would probably happen to us if we were to put any one of the beatitudes on a sign and walk down main street."

Reinhold Niebuhr says it another way: "Nothing which is true or beautiful or good makes complete sense in any immediate context of history: therefore we must be saved by faith."

John F. Kennedy observed, "War will exist until that distant day when the conscientious objector enjoys the same reputation and prestige that the warrior does today." A true peacemaker is not passive. He believes in the power of love and the power of God. "For though we live in the world, we do not wage war as the world does. The weapons we fight with are not the weapons of the world" (2 Corinthians 10:3, 4). The Christian peacemaker believes that no ruler is more powerful than God, and that God will finally triumph. The peacemaker gives priority to solving conflict at his own risk rather than at the risk of another. Jesus said, "Blessed are the peacemakers" not just the "peacekeepers."

6

The Christian Practice

6

The Christian Practice

Although my position does not arise from the traditional or historical approach, but from the Scripture, yet the facts of history are striking in speaking to the early Christians' attitudes toward war.

All serious scholars of church history today agree that for the first three centuries of the Christian church, Christians rejected not only emperor worship and idolatry but participation in the military. Obedience to the gospel, the early church held, was consistent only with a position of nonresistance and not serving in the military.

Yale church historian Roland Bainton writes, "From the end of the New Testament period to the decade 170-180 there is no evidence whatever of Christians in the army." Guy F. Hershberger adds, "It is quite clear that prior to about AD 174 it is impossible to speak of Christian soldiers." No single leader of Christianity in the pre-Constantinian era (313 AD) approved a military career as right for a believer in Jesus Christ. Bainton further says,

"All of the East and West repudiated participation in warfare for Christians." Later when some began to serve as secretaries, clerks, and other noncombatant positions in the military, the early church father, Tertullian, disagreed with this and any kind of participation.

Tertullian (who died in AD 225) asked, "If we are enjoined to love our enemies, who are we to hate? If injured we are forbidden to retaliate, who then can suffer injury at our hands?" Tertullian also insisted that if a soldier is converted he must immediately abandon the military (which he says many have done). Other early church fathers made similar statements.

Justin Martyr (martyred in AD 150) said, "We who were filled with war, and mutual slaughter, and every wickedness, have each through the whole earth changed our warlike weapons, our swords into ploughshares and our spears into implements of tillage."

Origen, the great Alexandrian theologian of a century later said, "We [Christians] no longer take up sword against nation, nor do we learn war any more, but are become the children of peace."

In March of AD 295 Maximilian, the son of an army officer, was put to death for refusal to put on a soldier's uniform. He refused to accept the soldier's badge saying repeatedly that he could not do so because he was a Christian. The story of his trial and his response and death is recorded in many books with clear evidence that he was considered by the church at that time as a holy martyr for refusing to serve in the military.

English scholar C. J. Cadoux, in his thorough and extensive study of the early church and war, says that the church testified uniformly against the military profession during the first three centuries of the Christian church. In

his book, *The Early Christian Attitude Toward War,*
Cadoux reports that early Christians did not compromise
on nonresistance; only after Constantine gave Christianity the official support of the empire was compromise
made. The writings of Augustine finally influenced the
church officially to sanction Christian participation in the
armies. G. J. Herring in *The Fall of Christianity* speaks of
this joining of church and state as the fall of the church.

In a substantial piece of historical scholarship, *It Is Not
Lawful for Me to Fight,* French scholar Jean-Michel
Hornus speaks of the great cover-up of the historical fact
that "all early Christians have agreed upon the rejection
of military violence." And one reason why this fact is
often overlooked is that this commitment "appears to
have been a spontaneous reaction by the Christians, a vir-
tual state of mind, rather than a dogma of a church law."
Hornus quotes the church fathers who stress the wrong-
ness for the Christian to go to war even when it appears
justified. He cites a soldier named Martin, converted
about the year 336 who was later Bishop of Tours. Martin
told the Emperor Julian, "Hitherto I have served you as a
soldier. Allow me now to become a soldier to God. Let the
man who is to serve you receive you donative. I am a
soldier of Christ. It is not lawful for me to fight."

Even many years later the church, at least in official
documents, opposed the Christian's engagement in warfare, which the following story illustrates.

When Ivan the Terrible ruled Russia, he was so intense
in his leadership that he neglected his social life. This became a great concern to his aides and upon their recom-
mendation Ivan decided to marry. He sent some of his
aides on a search for a bride. They settled on Sophia, the
daughter of the king of Greece. Ivan asked the king for

his daughter's hand. The wish was granted on the condition that Ivan the Terrible become a member of the Greek Orthodox Church, which he agreed to do.

Upon hearing of the church's requirements for baptism, Ivan was distressed. One of the articles stated that a member could no longer be a professional soldier. So Ivan devised a plan. When he and 500 of his army went into the water with 500 priests for baptism by immersion, Ivan and his soldiers each extended an arm, with a sword, out of the water. They had joined the church with their bodies but left their swords and fighting arms unbaptized.

How persistently the church has thought that it can own Christ's lordship and still kill with the sword. At least Ivan and his soldiers recognized the conflict and contradiction more clearly than most of Christendom through the centuries.

> *Whoever would love life*
> *and see good days*
> *must keep his tongue from evil*
> *and his lips from deceitful speech.*
> *He must turn from evil and do good;*
> *he must seek peace and pursue it.*

1 Peter 3:10, 11.

A
Peace Bibliography

A Peace Bibliography

Abrams, Ray H. *Preachers Present Arms*. Herald Press, 1969.
A documented story of the involvement of the church in three modern wars. It records the part which churches and the clergy have played. In showing preachers caught in the vortex of war madness, the author reveals the influence of war psychology, its propaganda techniques, uses of slogans, and manipulation of emotionally charged symbols. A Christian Peace Shelf selection.

Bales, James D. *The Christian Conscientious Objector*.
Deals with many of the questions people raise as to participation of the Christian in warfare.

Bender, Urie A. *Soldiers of Compassion*. Herald Press, 1969.
The story of young men from the United States who served in foreign countries in Voluntary Service in lieu of military service. Here is the report of persons from more than a score of countries all of whom have had a part in the story of Pax. In addition to the Paxmen's stories are the reports of refugees, doctors, government officials, farmers, teachers, community leaders, matrons, villagers, file clerks, administrators, nurses, children, and secretaries. *Pax*, the Latin word for peace, was chosen as the theme for this unique kind of service rendered by the church and Christians who believe there is a better way to solve world conflict than with the use of guns.

Berkhof, Hendrik. *Christ and the Powers*. Herald Press, 1977.
This translation from the Dutch by John Howard Yoder is a probing study of Paul's references to the "powers" in the epistles. The powers undergird creation, according to the author, becoming evil in their influence only as they seek dominion for themselves.

Brown, Dale W. *Brethren and Pacifism*. Brethren Press, 1970.
Discusses the Brethren response to war. Also speaks to the "what if" questions people raise.

Church Peace Mission Pamphlets. Herald Press.
This series of pamphlets published by the Church Peace Mission deals with the issues of war, the ethics of Christianity, and the relationships between the two. The pamphlets clarify issues and give perspective to the questions. All were designed to contribute to dialogue within the church.

The Christian Conscience and War, John Oliver Nelson
The Christian Church and National Ethos, John Smylie
The Mission of the Church and Civil Government,
    Clinton Morrison
The Pacifism of Karl Barth, John H. Yoder
Reinhold Niebuhr and Christian Pacifism, John H. Yoder
Your Church and Your Nation, Paul Peachey

Detweiler, Richard C. *Mennonite Statements on Peace*.
Herald Press, 1968.
A study of the peace documents issued by the Mennonite Church from the beginning to the present day. Reveals the trends in thought and approach to the subject.

Driver, John. *Kingdom Citizens*. Herald Press, 1980.
Designed to orient direct study of the Sermon on the Mount. For those who desire a life of discipleship which corresponds more nearly to God's intention for his community of salvation.

Durland, William R. *No King But Caesar?* Herald Press, 1975.
A Catholic lawyer examines biblical teachings about nonresistance. Durland reviews the teachings of Jesus and the writings of the early church fathers. He traces the church's attitude toward violence through the centuries. A Christian Peace Shelf selection.

A *Peace Bibliography*

Eller, Vernard. *War and Peace from Genesis to Revelation*.
Herald Press, 1981.
Explores peace as a constant theme developing throughout the
Old and New Testaments. A Christian Peace Shelf selection.

Enz, Jacob. *The Christian and Warfare*. Herald Press, 1972.
The objective of the author is not to formulate a biblical doctrine
of pacifism but to reexamine the biblical concepts to see just what
is there. The author uses the gospel formula for interpreting and
applying the Word of life. The Old Testament Scriptures come to
life as they reveal again God's purpose and desire for mankind. A
Christian Peace Shelf selection.

Epp, Frank. *A Strategy for Peace*. Eerdmans.
Reflections by a historian on war and peace. The unrealism of
militarism and the church and nationalism are dealt with. A dialogue between pacifists and nonpacifists.

Fast, H. A. *Jesus and Human Conflict*. Herald Press, 1959.
An easily read but penetrating study of Scripture dealing with the
Christian's response to political, religious, domestic, and personal
aggression. Here you will see what the everyday character and attitude should be for the person in whom the rule of God has become a living, working reality. A valuable and fresh source material for study groups.

Friesen, Ivan and Rachel. Shalom Pamphlets. Herald Press, 1981.
Six booklets intended to help young people relate Christian faith
to questions of war and peace. Written in a lively style with real-
life illustrations of people who have chosen to walk in the way of
peace.

Why Is Peace Missing?
What Is a Christian?
What Did Jesus Teach Us?
What Has the Church Done?
What Are the Issues?
How Do You Decide?

Funk, Jacob. *War Versus Peace*. Brethren Publishing House.
Deals with the causes, evils, and cost of war: a history of the peace
movement and ways of advancing peace.

Gingerich, Melvin. *Service for Peace*. Mennonite Central Committee, 1949.
A volume which speaks to the many ways conscientious objectors have served for peace from the American Revolution until today.

_____ *The Christian and Revolution*. Herald Press, 1968.
In a day of new nationalism, race revolution, and the threat of extremism of both the left-wing and right-wing varieties, how can Christians become truly agents of reconciliation? How does the Christian insulate himself from the propaganda of hatred? How does the Christian with social concerns avoid being swallowed up in the very thing he is trying to correct? The author believes the Christian should use the norms of the New Testament gospel in evaluating these forces and chart a course accordingly. A Conrad Grebel Lecture Series book.

Hartzler, J. S. *Mennonites in the World War*. Ozer, 1972.
Nonresistance under test. A report of how Mennonites responded to World War I.

Hershberger, Guy F. *The Mennonite Church in the Second World War*.
A report on how Mennonites responded to World War II.

_____ *War, Peace, and Nonresistance*. Herald Press, 1969.
A comprehensive work on nonresistance, its application and practice by the church through history. Biblical nonresistance and modern pacifism are analyzed and contrasted. Practical suggestions are given for a vigorous program of teaching and practice. Included is a discussion of the broad social implications of nonresistance. A Christian Peace Shelf selection.

Heuvel, Albert H. Van den. *These Religious Powers*. Friendship Press, 1965.
What are the powers which really mold our time? The author discusses the Christian's participation in the complexities of today's world, visible and invisible powers.

Hornus, Jean-Michel. *It Is Not Lawful for Me to Fight: Early Christian Attitudes Toward War, Violence, and the State*. Herald Press, 1980.
An outstanding book of research and study attempting to prove

that from the beginning and throughout the first three centuries the church was vigorously opposed to Christian participation in military service. He explains love, and how and why this position was abandoned during the fourth century. A Christian Peace Shelf selection.

Hostetler, Paul, editor. *Perfect Love and War*. Evangel Press.
A dialogue on issues of war and peace between many persons of differing opinions. Composed of papers written and presented at a peace conference.

Jacobs, Donald R. *The Christian Stance in a Revolutionary Age*. Herald Press, 1968.
The author discusses the question, "How does a Christian face the revolutionary changes in society which come peaceably and/or with violence in a developing country?" The question is raised to provide help to the Christians in Africa. Provides insights into the same problems in America.

Kaufman, Donald D. *The Tax Dilemma: Praying for Peace, Paying for War*. Herald Press, 1978.
One of the most complete treatments of the war tax issue. The author explores the moral implications for persons conscientiously opposed to war paying taxes to support the military. Traces biblical and historical precedents and discusses possible responses today. A Christian Peace Shelf selection.

_____. *What Belongs to Caesar?* Herald Press, 1969.
The author questions the responsibility Christians have to give to the government its tax demands for war. He examines biblical passages like "Render to Caesar" and then presents three basic arguments against voluntary payment of war taxes. A Christian Peace Shelf selection.

Kniss, Lloy A. *I Couldn't Fight*. Herald Press, 1971.
The personal testimony of one who couldn't fight in World War I. The author shares his beliefs and the outcome of putting them into practice.

Kraybill, Donald B. *Our Star-Spangled Faith*. Herald Press, 1976.
Looks at civil religion in America, the marriage of politics and piety. Written for the interested layman. He makes a plea for a

faith that moves beyond America's "God and country" religion or a patriotism which pursues love, justice, and mercy for all mankind. Introduction by Martin E. Marty.

Lapp, John A. *A Dream for America*. Herald Press, 1976.
Christian reflections for Bicentennial reading. Presented are some of the issues that are critical to community and national survival if there are to be future centennial celebrations. Americans need to understand the times to know what needs to be done. Introduction by U.S. Senator Mark Hatfield.

Lasserre, Jean. *War and the Gospel*. Herald Press, 1962.
A book for those with questions concerning the extent to which a Christian can or should participate in warfare. Defense of country, responsibility to the state, the lordship of Christ, the sixth commandment, and responsibility for the brother are a few of the subjects discussed. First published in French, then German, and now available in the English language. The author, a Frenchman, has made an important contribution to the subject. Herald Press is the distributor in North America. Eighteen pages of reference and seven pages of bibliography. A Christian Peace Shelf selection.

Lehn, Cornelia. *Peace Be with You*. Faith and Life Press, 1981.
Stories about people who "dared to live and die for their faith, people all through the centuries who had taken Christ seriously." A resource for ministers, parents, and teachers to help share the Christian way of peace.

Lind, Millard C. *Yahweh Is a Warrior*. Herald Press, 1980.
A systematic scholarly reexamination of the biblical material on warfare in ancient Israel. A Christian Peace Shelf selection.

McSorley, Richard. *Kill? for Peace?* Corpus Books, 1970.
A priest argues that modern warfare is so destructive that it cannot be defended on moral grounds. Filled with facts; hits hard at human survival.

Miller, John W. *The Christian Way*. Herald Press, 1969.
A guide to the Christian life based on the Sermon on the Mount. A Christian Peace Shelf selection.

Miller, Melissa, and Phil M. Shenk. *The Path of Most Resistance*. Herald Press, 1982.
Stories of Mennonite conscientious objectors who did not cooperate with the Vietnam War draft.

Peachey, J. Lorne. *How to Teach Peace to Children*.
Herald Press, 1981.
Twenty-one ideas gleaned from Mennonite, Quaker, and Brethren publications since World War II.

Ramseyer, Robert, editor. *Mission and the Peace Witness*.
Herald Press, 1979.
This book presents peace and reconciliation as an integral part of the gospel message. Seven experienced church leaders and scholars bring together biblical, historical, theological, and missiological perspectives on this theme. Contributors include: John H. Yoder, Robert Ramseyer, Richard Showalter, Ronald J. Sider, Sjouke Voolstra, Marlin E. Miller, and James Metzler. Mennonite Missionary Study Series, No. 7.

Redekop, John H. *Making Political Decisions*. Herald Press, 1972.
The author presents the options available and emphasizes that each Christian must accept the responsibility for his actions or inaction on issues.

Roth, Willard. Peacemaker Pamphlets. Herald Press, 1964.
A series of booklets which clarify the Christian's responsibility to the state, to God, and to himself. These books are designed to help the teenager face a modern world and all its pressures to conform to the status quo. Written for those who are able to think.

Why Do Men Fight?
Why Be a Christian?
What Does Christ Say About War?
What About Church History?
Is There a Middle Road?
What Is Christian Citizenship?

Rutenber, Culbert G. *The Dagger and the Cross*.
Fellowship Publications, 1950.
An excellent book by a professor of the philosophy of religions at

Eastern Baptist. Written when not much material on this subject was being produced by persons from nonpacifist denominations.

Sider, Ronald J. *Christ and Violence*. Herald Press, 1979.
A book which looks to Jesus for an example of how to respond to the violent world in which we live. Both persons who think they can have Christ without pacifism and those who think they can have pacifism without Christ will have to think again after reading this book. A Christian Peace Shelf selection.

Steiner, Susan Clemmer. *Joining the Army That Sheds No Blood*. Herald Press, 1982.
Directed to youth. Sets forth the biblical basis for pacifism in the context of the issues facing North American teenagers in the 1980s. A Christian Peace Shelf selection.

Trocmé, André. *Jesus and the Nonviolent Revolution*. Herald Press, 1974.
Trocmé presents Jesus Christ as a vigorous revolutionary who changes the world nonviolently through love. This book examines and elaborates on the ways he carries out his revolution. Appropriate for study groups. A Christian Peace Shelf selection.

Wenger, J. C. *Pacifism and Biblical Nonresistance*. Herald Press, 1968.
A history of biblical nonresistance and a discussion of the difference between pacifism and biblical nonresistance.

_____ *The Way of Peace*. Herald Press, 1977.
The author sets forth Christ's teachings on love. He traces this way of peace through the centuries. He shows what it can and should mean in the life of the Christian and how it relates to persons in conflict.

Yoder, John H. *Nevertheless*. Herald Press, 1972.
The author examines the varieties and shortcomings of religious pacifism, clarifying the many-sided conversation about war. Provides for a greater awareness of the gamut of varying and even contradictory views of pacifism. Instead of debating the rights and the wrongs, the author summarizes what each position says and assumes. A Christian Peace Shelf selection.

_____ *The Original Revolution*. Herald Press, 1972.

Emphasizes that the renunciation of the sword is one of the keys to the problem of Christian faithfulness and to the recovery of the evangelical integrity of the church. Written to the Christian who has become aware of the problem of war and inadequate moral guidance that has been given by the church in the past. A Christian Peace Shelf selection.

The
Author

John M. Drescher, Harrisonburg, Virginia, was born
and grew up near Lancaster, Pennsylvania. He attended
Elizabethtown College, Eastern Mennonite College, and
Goshen Biblical Seminary. He is married to Betty Keener
and they are parents of three boys and two girls ages 27 to
17.

From 1954 to 1962 Drescher served as pastor in Ohio.
In 1962 he was called to edit *Gospel Herald*, the official
organ of the Mennonite Church. In 1973 he became pastor of the Scottdale Mennonite Church, Scottdale, Pennsylvania.

Since 1979 he is teacher at Eastern Mennonite
Seminary in the areas of preaching, integration of
theology, and spiritual disciplines, and he is speaker for
the Sunday morning student worship at Eastern Mennonite College.

Drescher served as assistant moderator and moderator
of the Mennonite Church and on the board of the

Associated Church Press. He has authored 25 books among which are *Seven Things Children Need, If I Were Starting My Family Again, Now Is the Time to Love, Spirit Fruit, When Opposites Attract, When You Think You Are in Love,* and *Meditations for the Newly Married.*

Drescher has written for more than 100 different magazines and journals including *Reader's Digest, Christianity Today, The Ministry, Catholic Digest, Moody Monthly,* and *Decision.* A number of his books have been translated into other languages including Japanese, Chinese, Thai, Spanish, German, Dutch, and French.

He is a contributing editor to *Pulpit Digest* and has served across denominational lines in conventions, retreats, and seminars—particularly in the area of Christian family life.

The Christian Peace Shelf

The Christian Peace Shelf is a selection of Herald Press books and pamphlets devoted to the promotion of Christian peace principles and their applications. The editor (appointed by the Mennonite Central Committee Peace Section) and an editorial board from the Brethren in Christ Church, the General Conference Mennonite Church, the Mennonite Brethren Church, and the Mennonite Church represent the historic concern for peace within these constituencies.

FOR SERIOUS STUDY

Abrams, Ray H. *Preachers Present Arms* (1969). The involvement of the church in three modern wars.

Durland, William R. *No King but Caesar?* (1975). A Catholic lawyer looks at Christian violence.

Enz, Jacob J. *The Christian and Warfare* (1972). The roots of pacifism in the Old Testament.

Hershberger, Guy F. *War, Peace, and Nonresistance* (Third Edition, 1969). A classic comprehensive work on nonresistance in faith and history.

Hornus, Jean-Michael. *It Is Not Lawful for Me to Fight* (1980). Early Christian attitudes toward war, violence, and the state.

Kaufman, Donald D. *What Belongs to Caesar?* (1969). Basic arguments against voluntary payment of war taxes.

Lasserre, Jean. *War and the Gospel* (1962). An analysis of Scriptures related to the ethical problem of war.

Lind, Millard C. *Yahweh is a Warrior* (1980). The theology of warfare in ancient Israel.

Ramseyer, Robert L. *Mission and the Peace Witness* (1979). Implications of the biblical peace testimony for the evangelizing mission of the church.

Sider, Ronald J. *Christ and Violence* (1979). A sweeping reappraisal of the church's teaching on violence.

Trocmé, André. *Jesus and the Nonviolent Revolution* (1973). The social and political relevance of Jesus.

Yoder, John H. *The Original Revolution* (1972). Essays on Christian pacifism.

_____ *Nevertheless* (1971). The varieties and shortcomings of Christian pacifism.

FOR EASY READING

Drescher, John M, *Why I Am a Conscientious Objector* (1982). A personal summary of basic issues for every Christian facing military involvements.

Eller, Vernard. *War and Peace from Genesis to Revelation* (1981). Explores peace as a consistent theme developing throughout the Old and New Testaments.

Kaufman, Donald D. *The Tax Dilemma: Praying for Peace, Paying for War* (1978). Biblical, historical, and practical considerations on the war tax issue.

Kraybill, Donald B. *The Upside-Down Kingdom* (1978). A study of the synoptic gospels on affluence, war-making, status-seeking, and religious exclusivism.

Miller, John W. *The Christian Way* (1969). A guide to the Christian life based on the Sermon on the Mount.

Steiner, Susan Clemmer. *Joining the Army That Sheds No Blood* (1982). The case for biblical pacifism written for teens.

Wenger, J. C. *The Way of Peace* (1977). A brief treatment on Christ's teachings and the way of peace through the centuries.

FOR CHILDREN

Bauman, Elizabeth Hershberger. *Coals of Fire* (1954). Stories of people who returned good for evil.

Moore, Ruth Nulton. *Peace Treaty* (1977). A historical novel involving the efforts of Moravian missionary Christian Frederick Post to bring peace to the Ohio Valley in 1758.

Smucker, Barbara Claassen. *Henry's Red Sea* (1955). The dramatic escape of 1,000 Russian Mennonites from Berlin following World War II.